Very SCARY MOMENTS Coloring Book

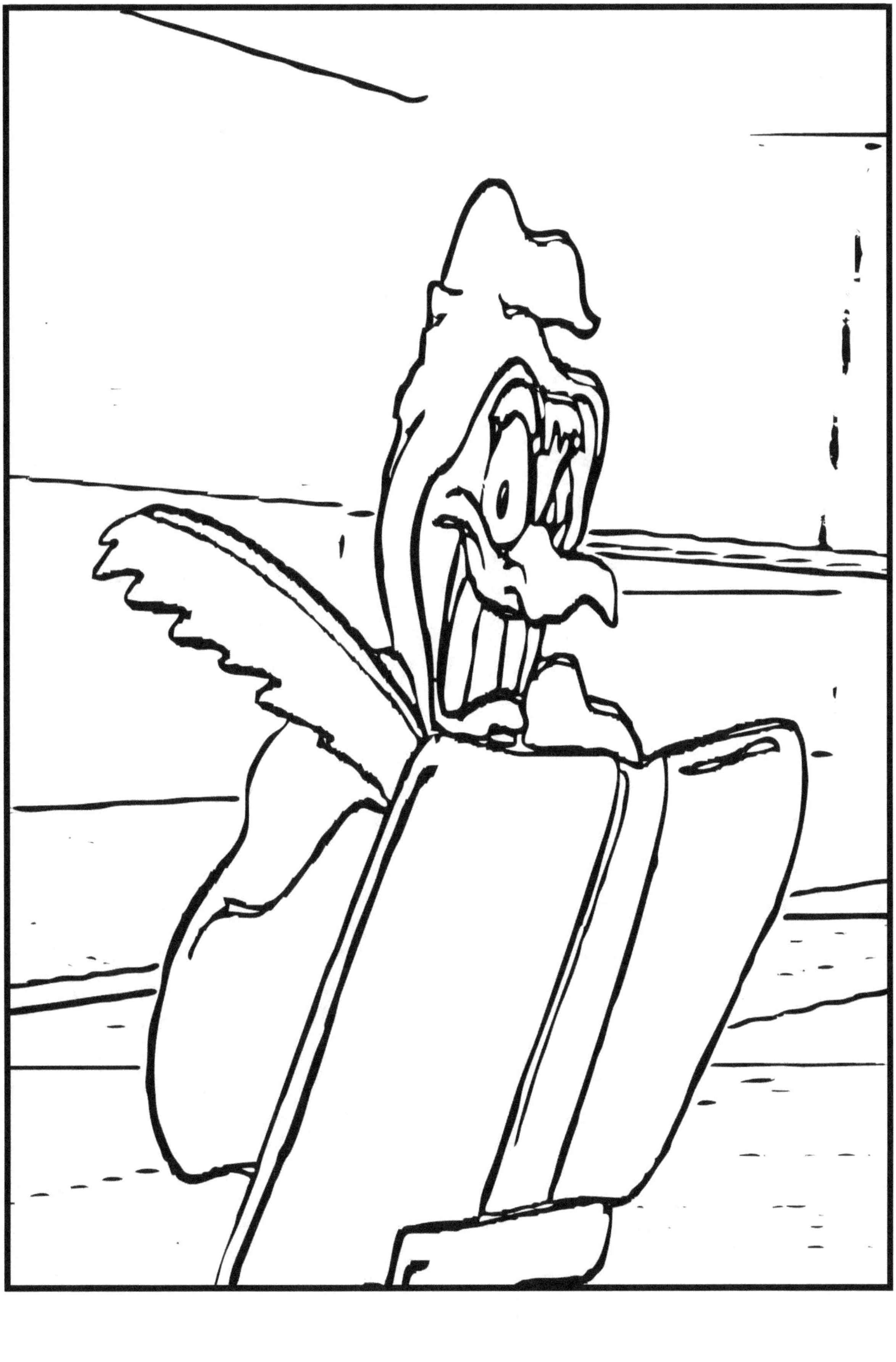

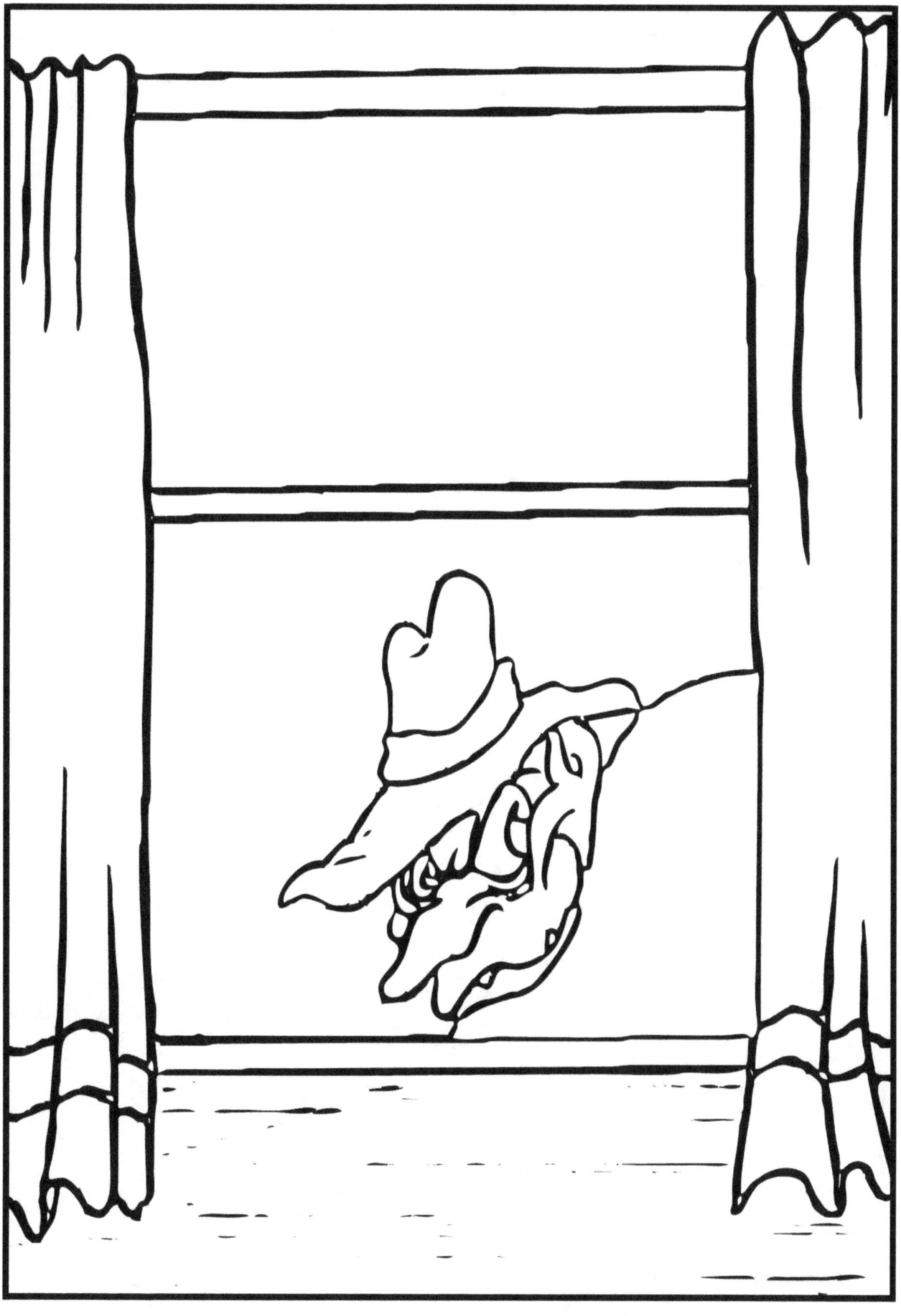

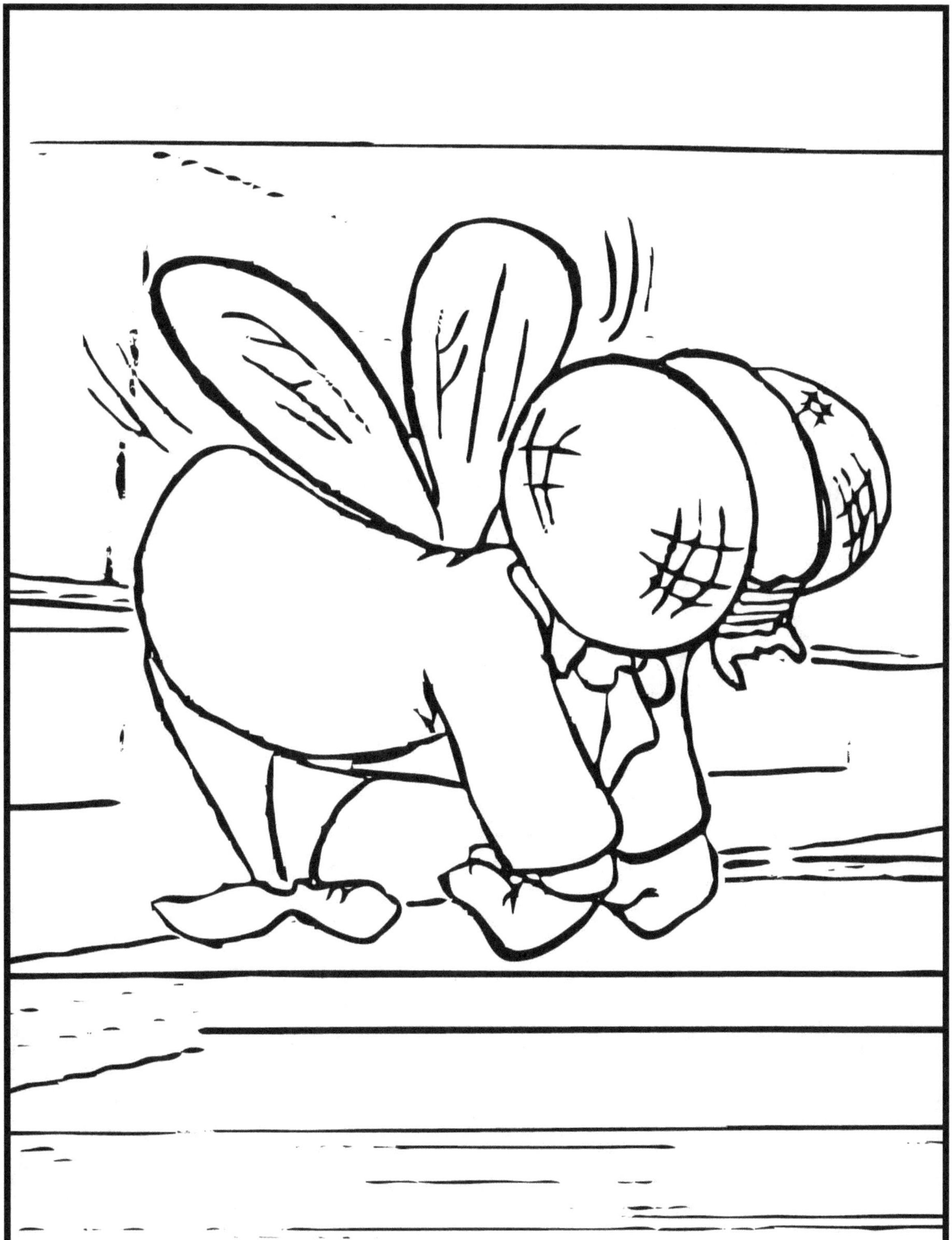

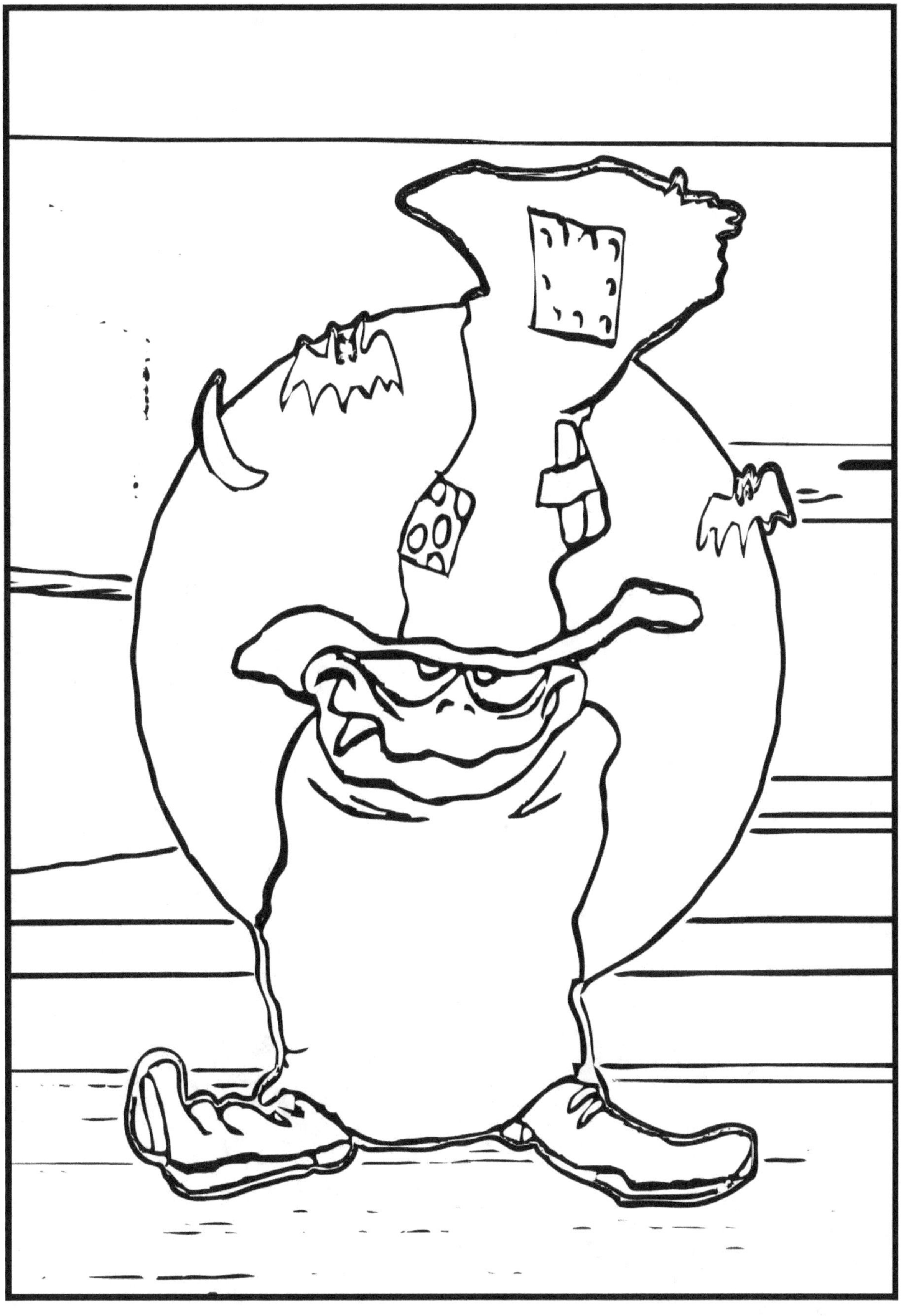

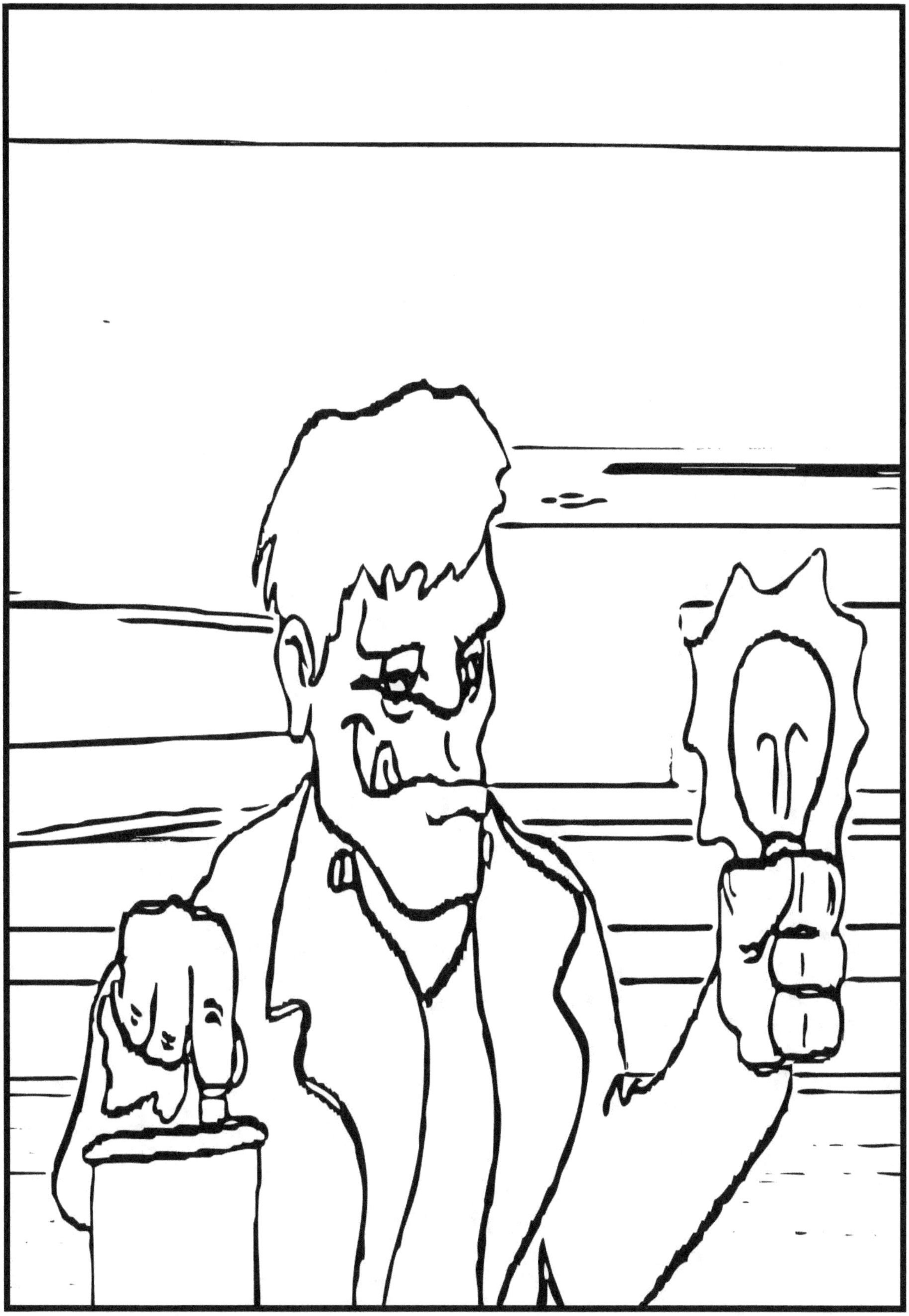

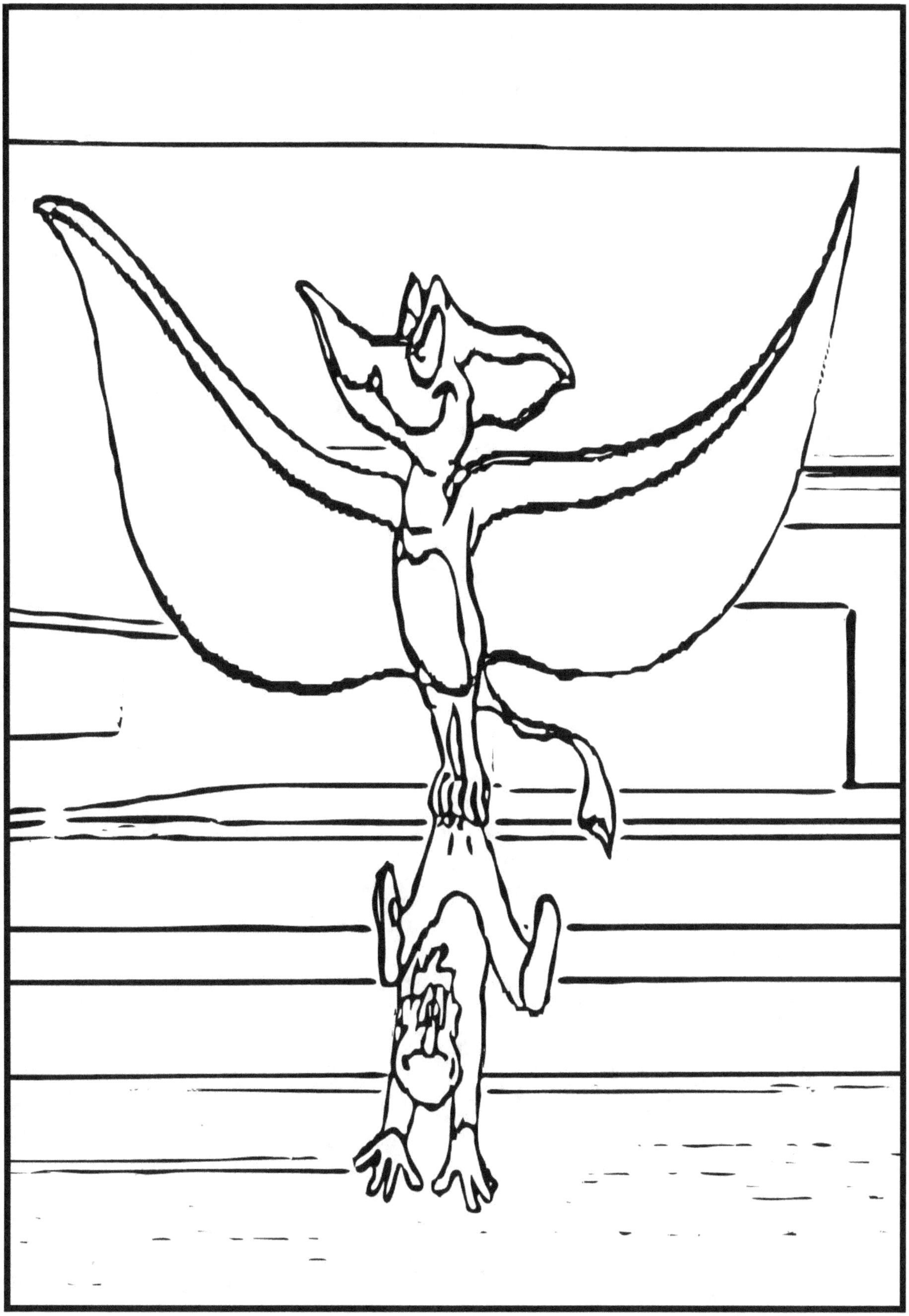

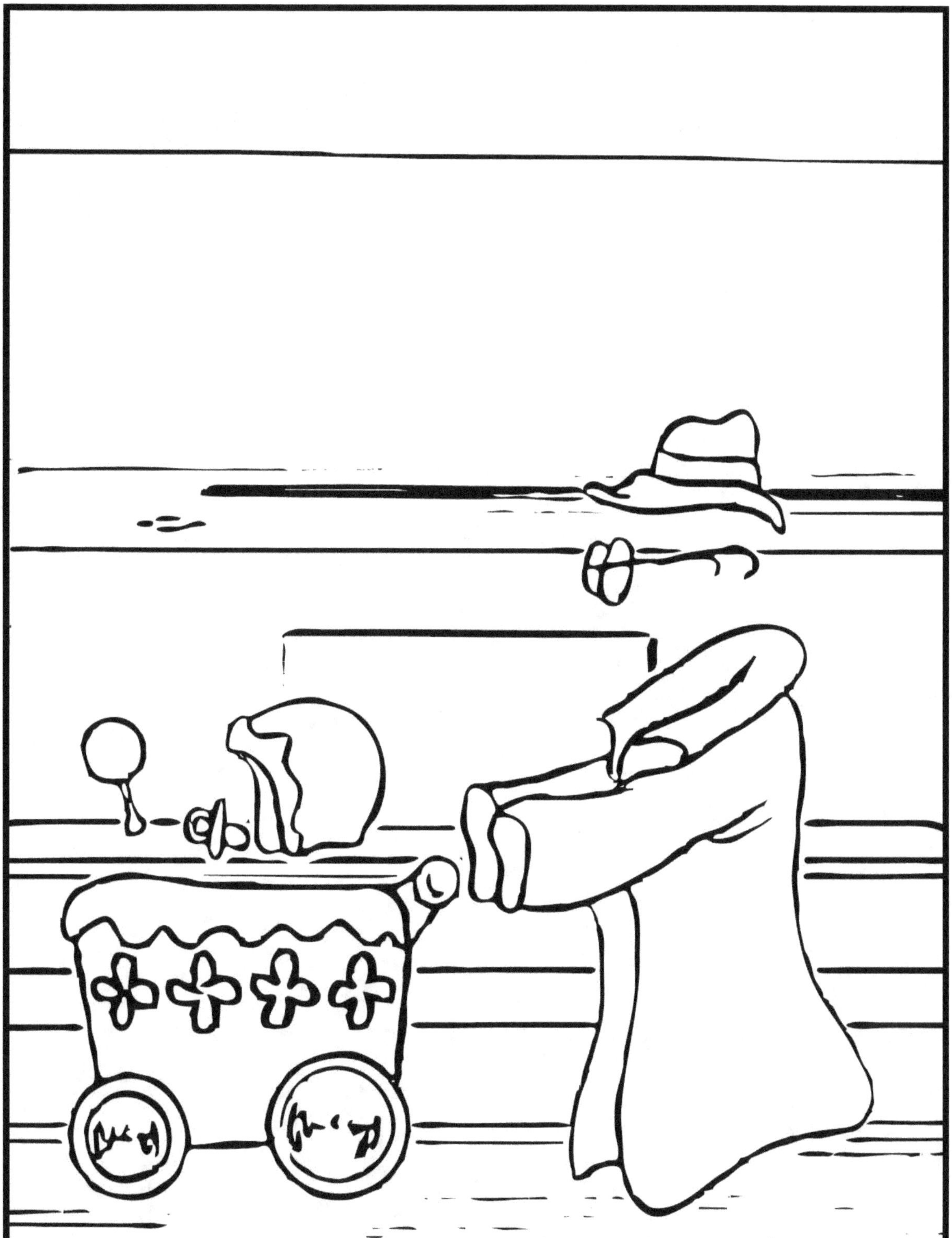

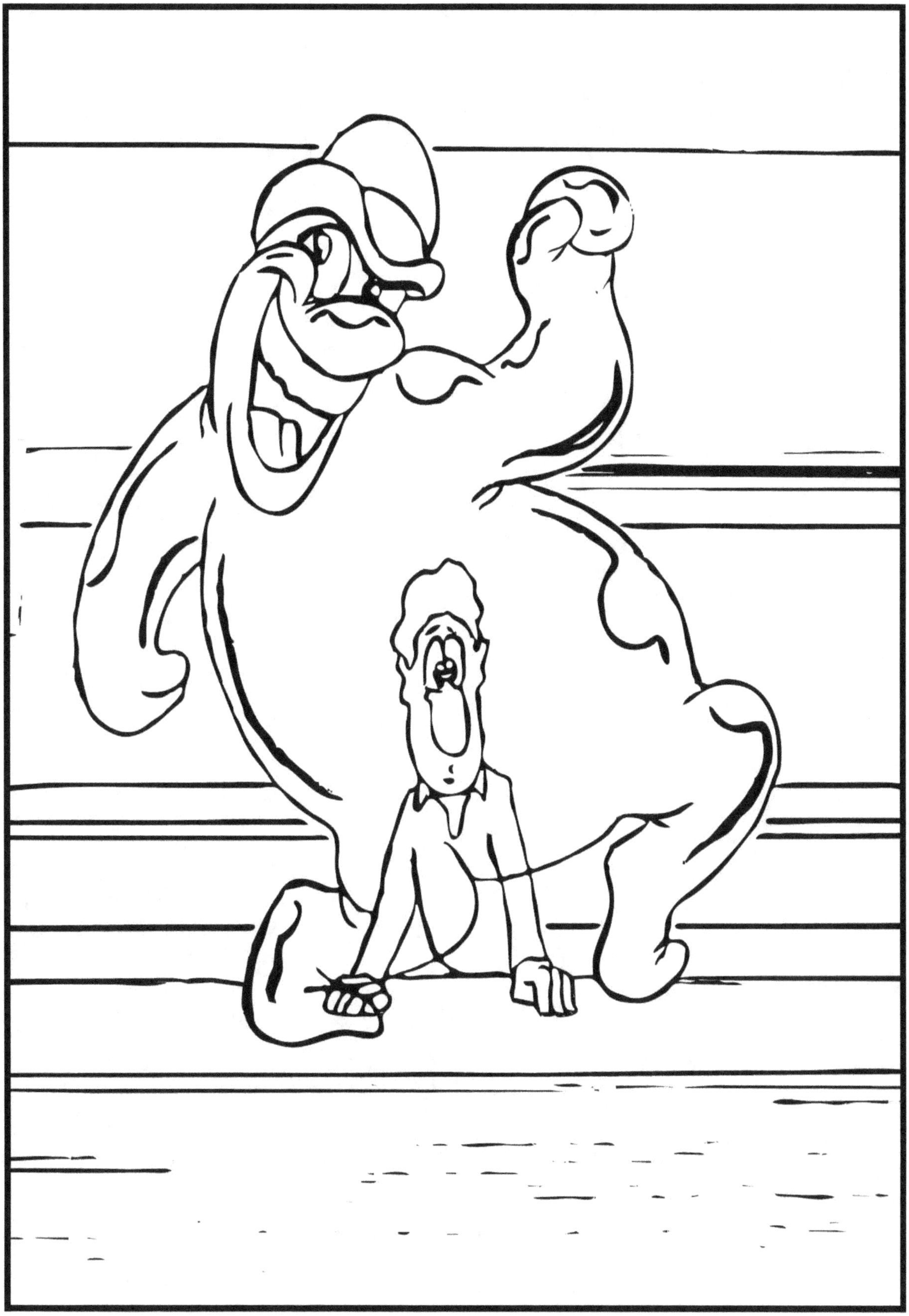

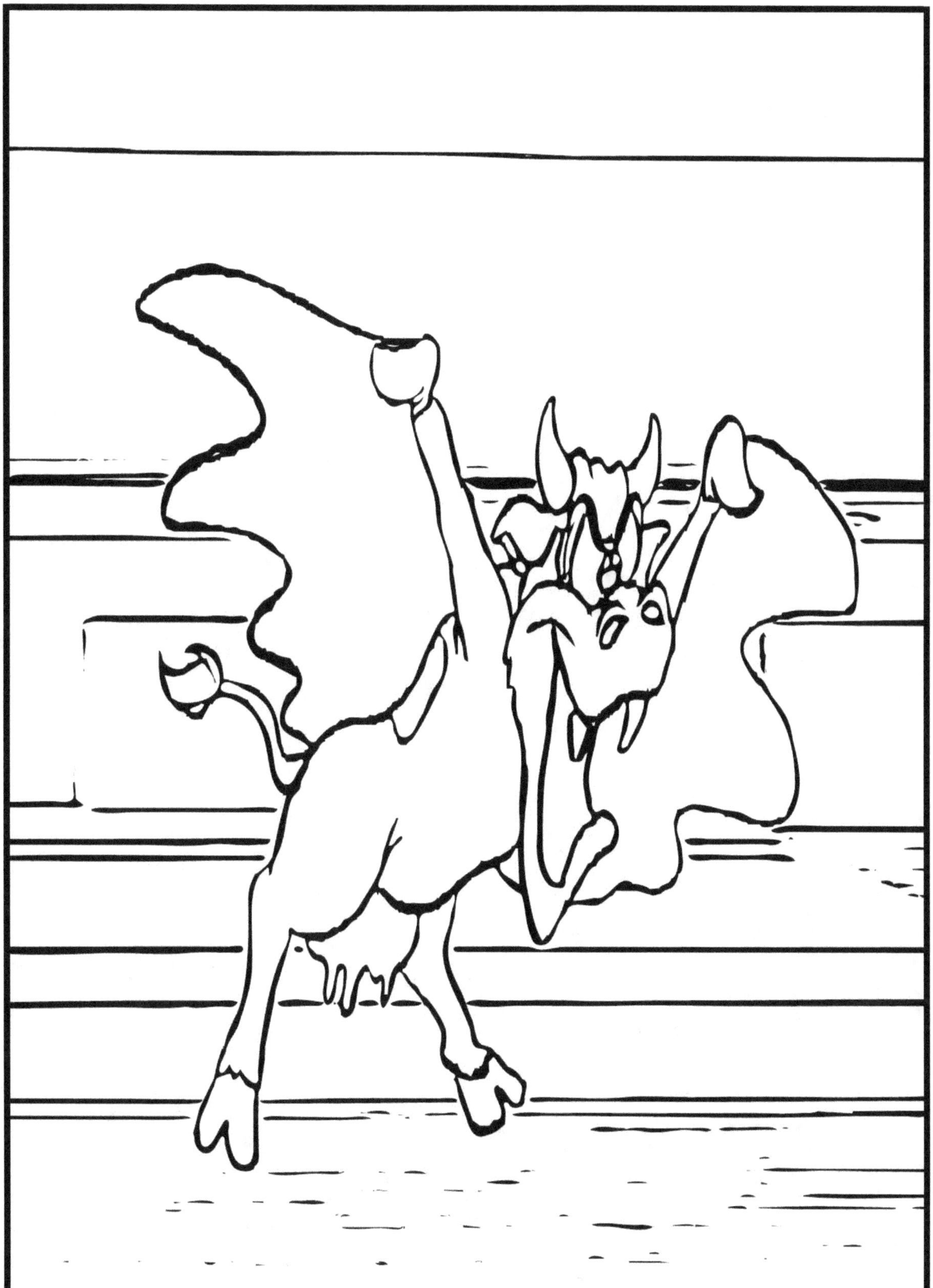

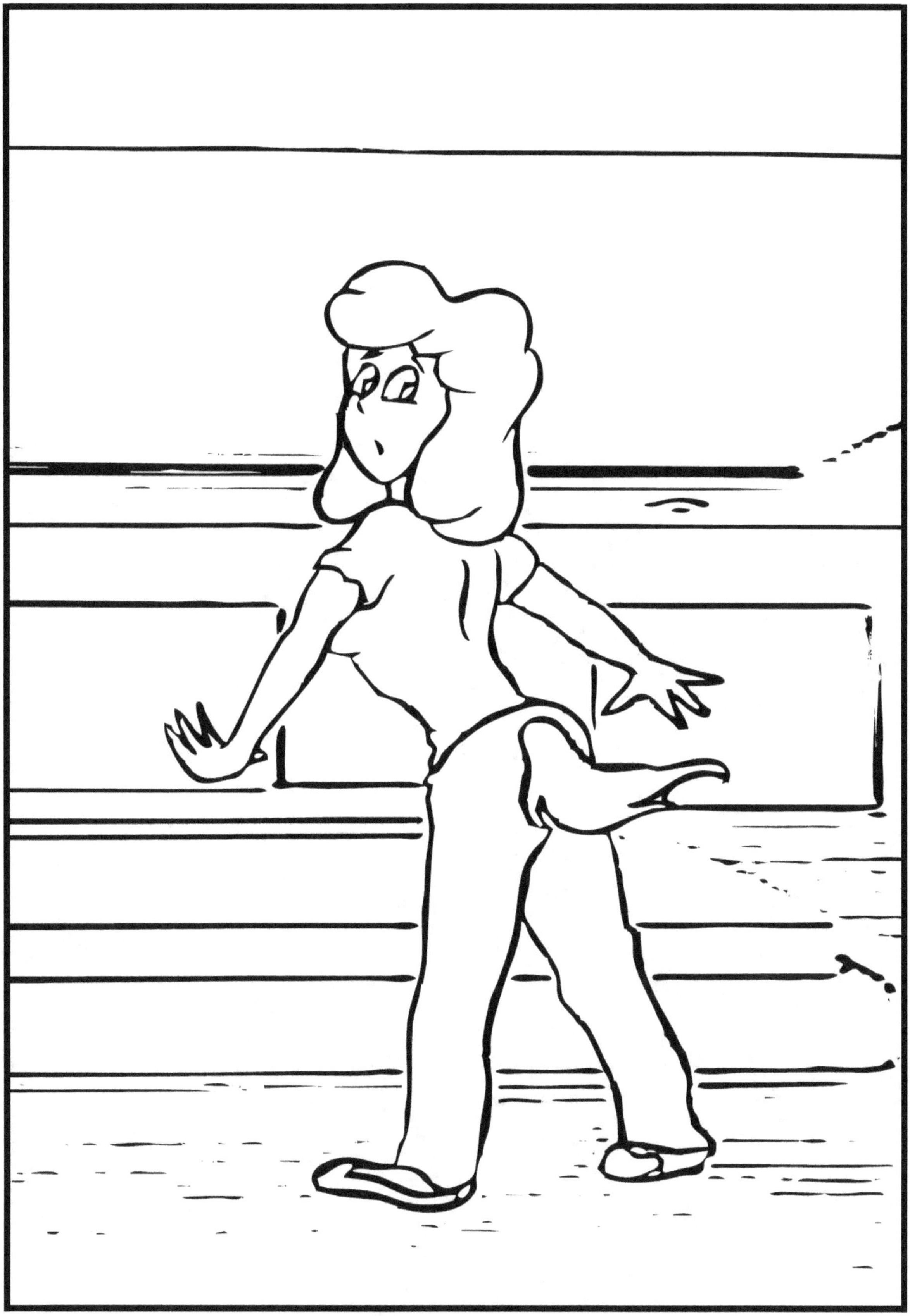

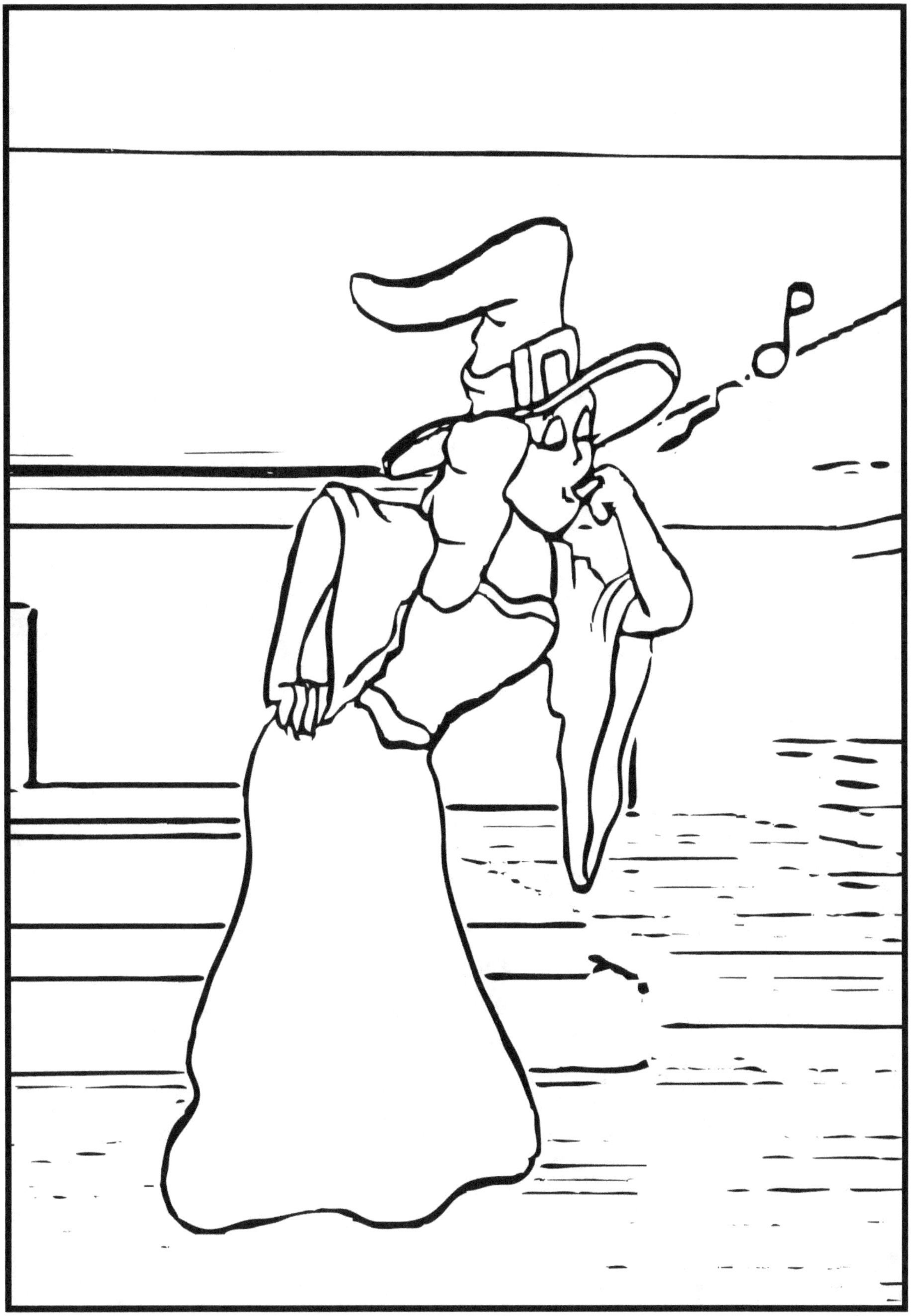

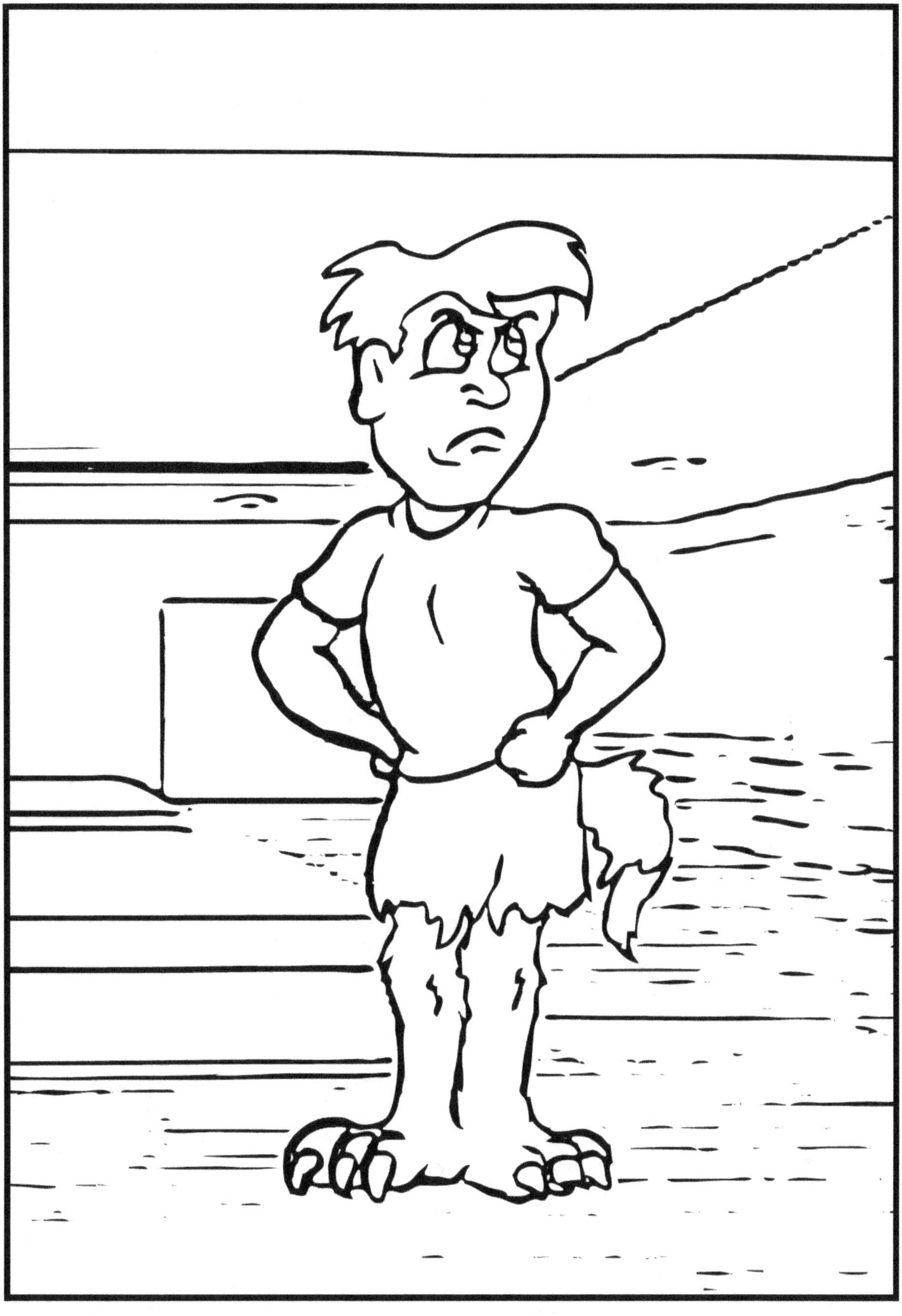

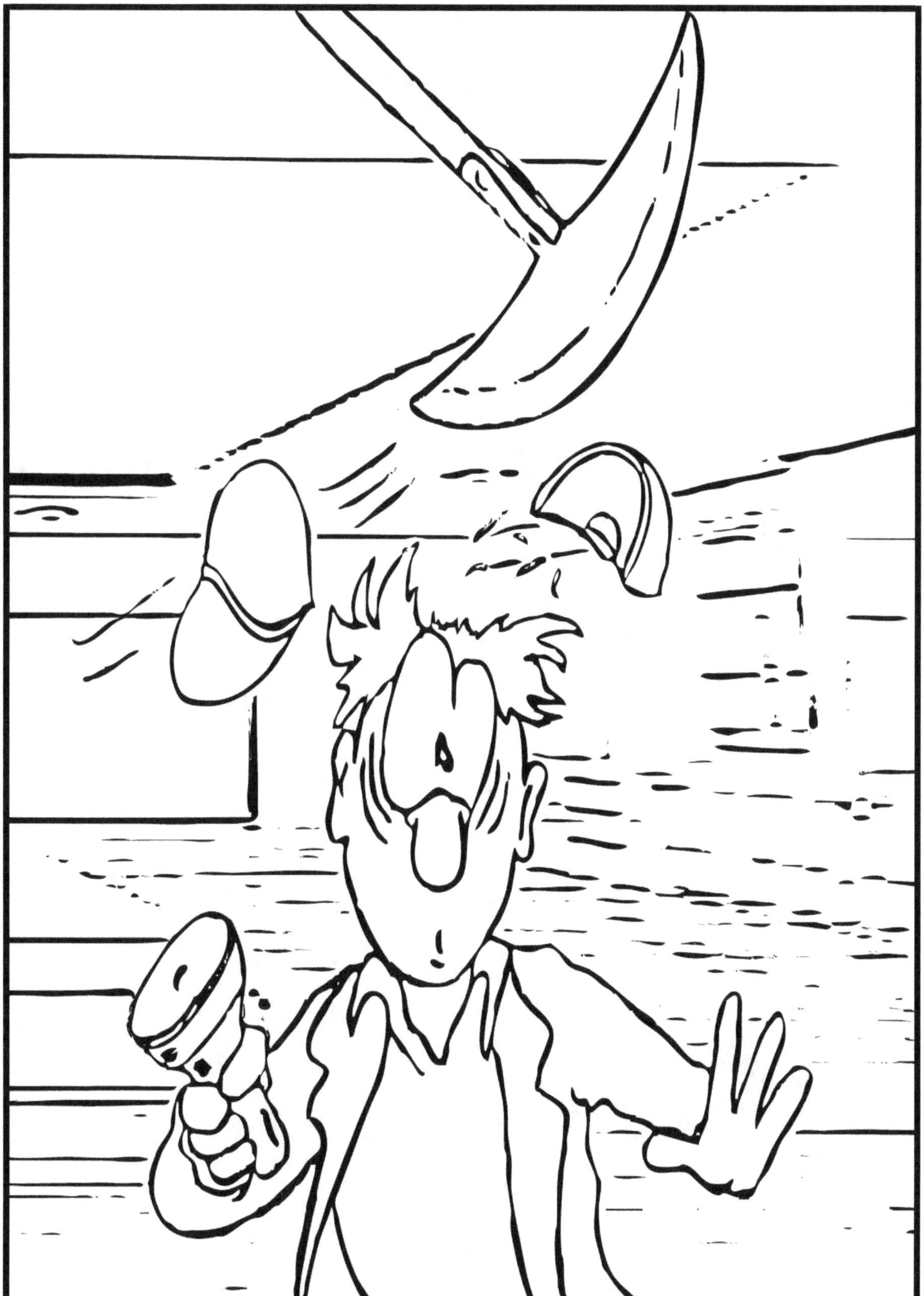

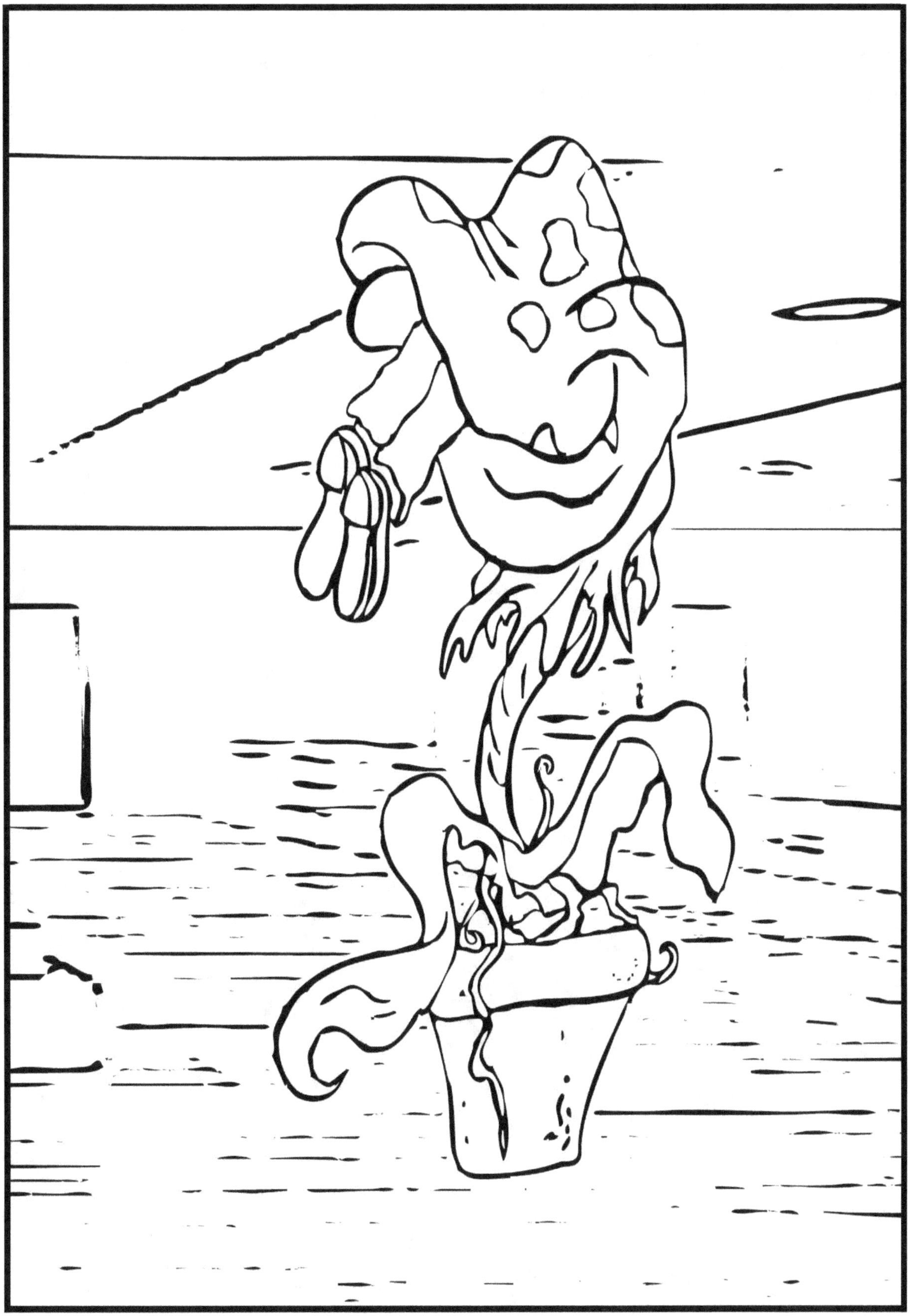

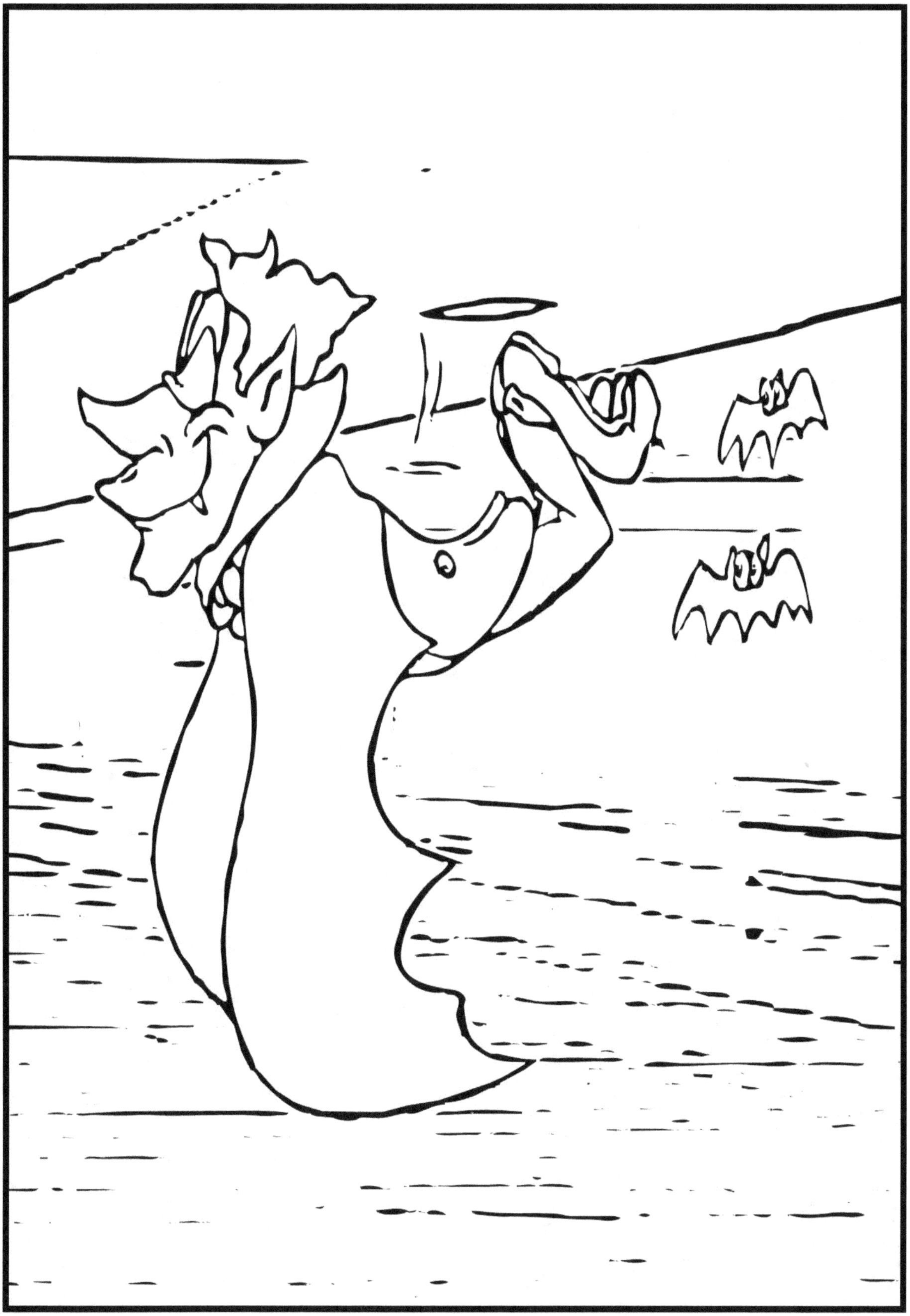

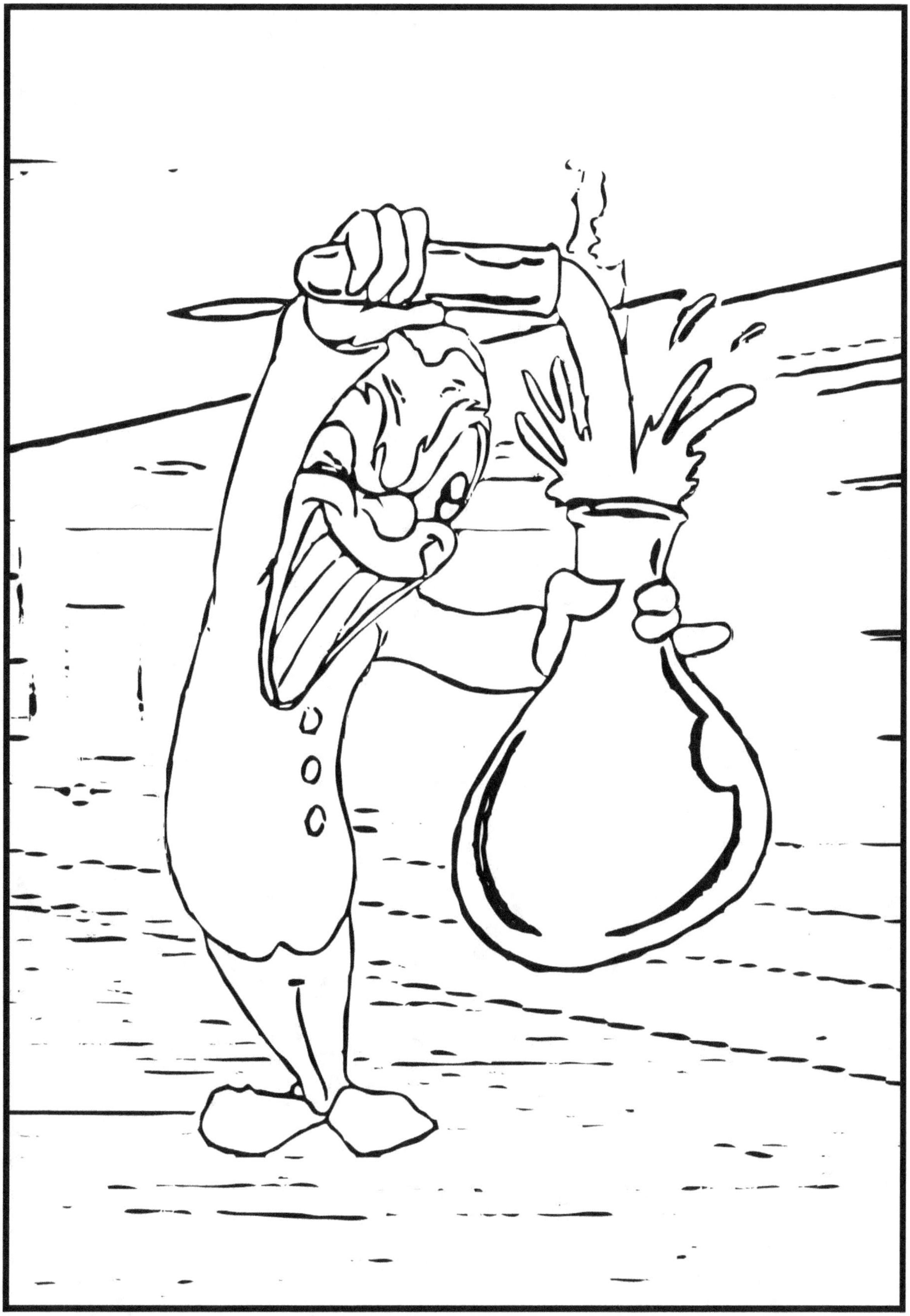

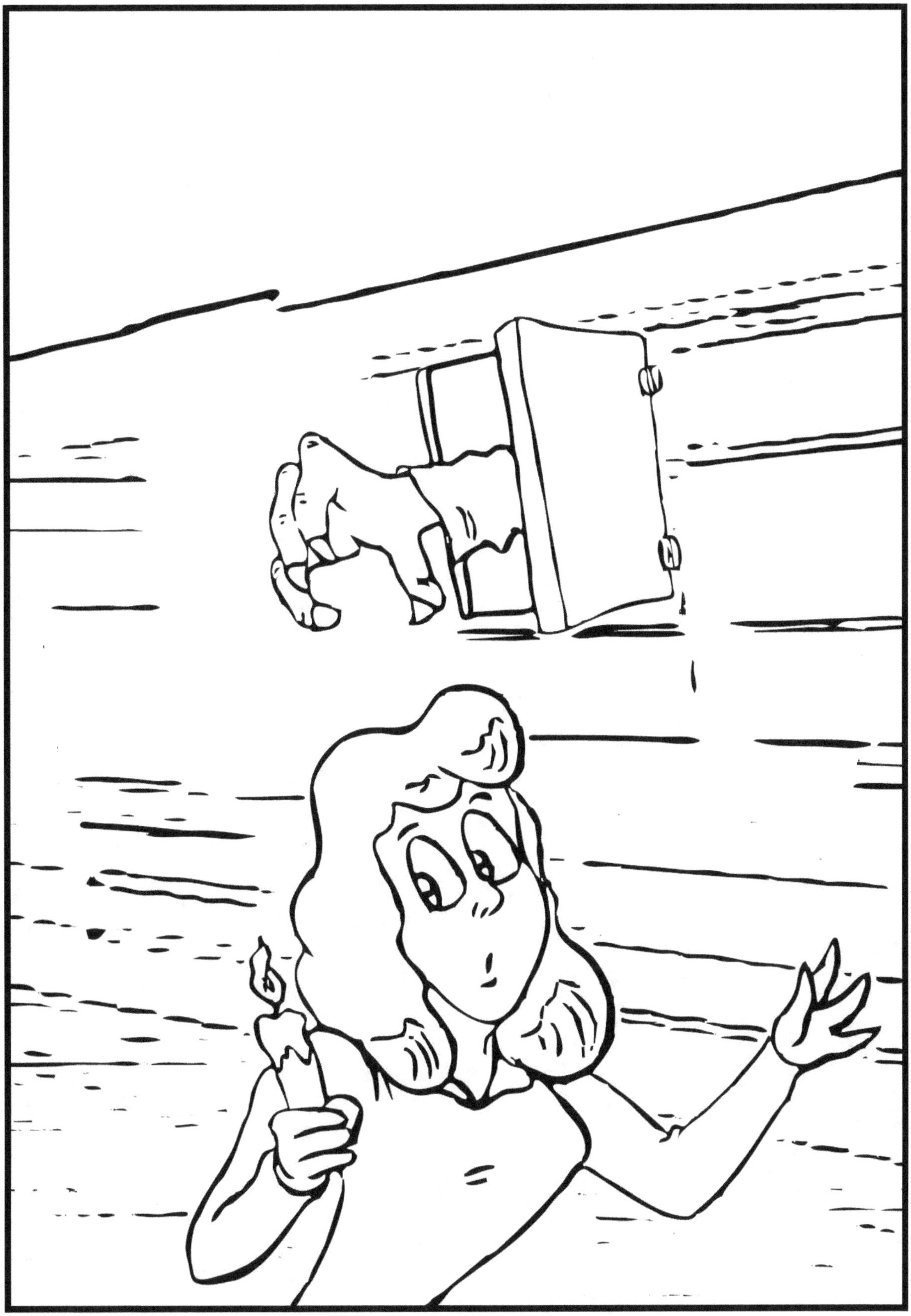

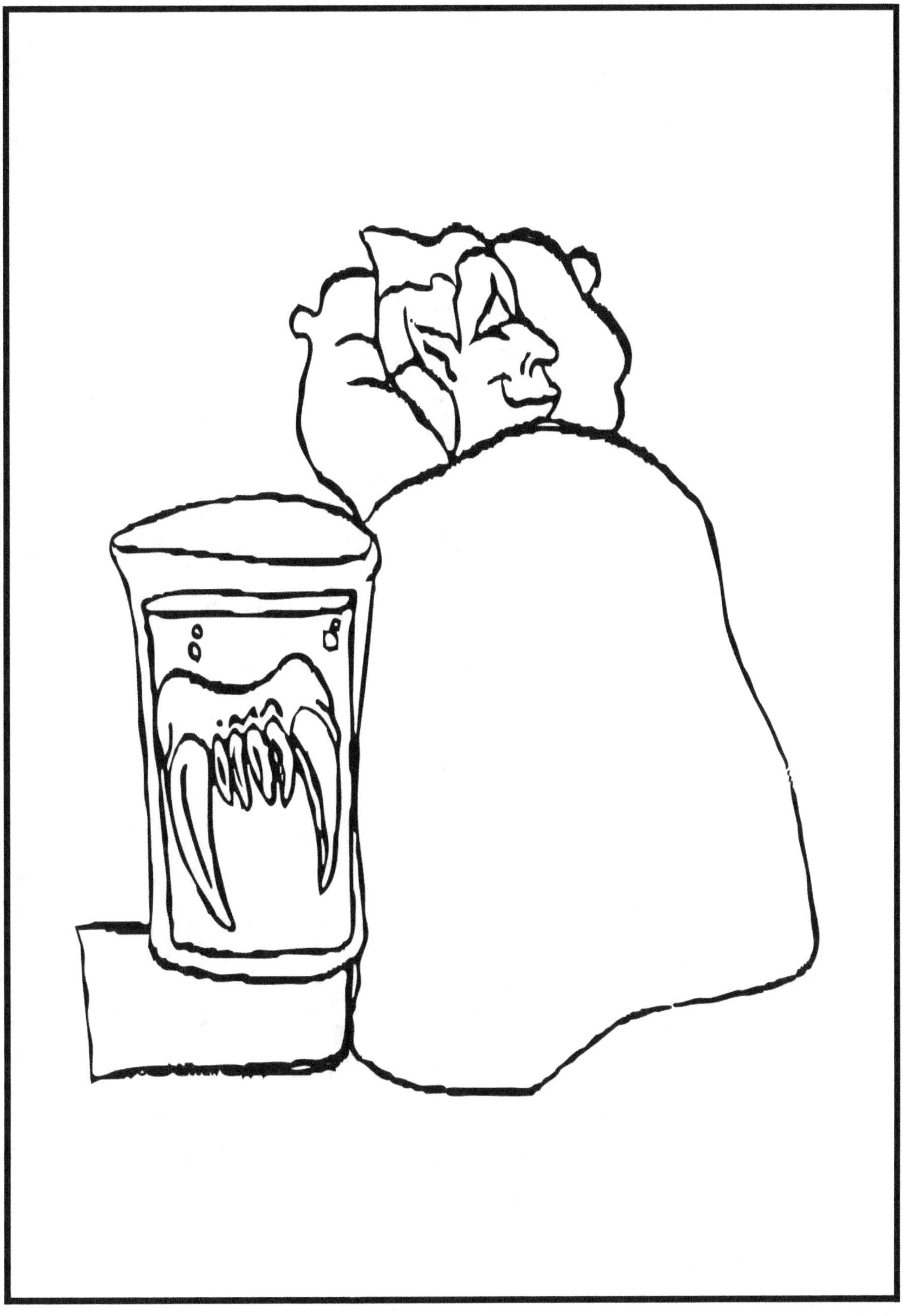

www.ingramcontent.com/pod-product-compliance
Lightning Source LLC
Chambersburg PA
CBHW081311180526
45170CB00007B/2662
9781522869559